HUMAN ESSAYS

Human Essays

Conscripted Poems 1971-2021

Paul Gillespie

Columbus, Ohio

The views and opinions expressed in this book are solely those of the author and do not reflect the views or opinions of Gatekeeper Press. Gatekeeper Press is not to be held responsible for and expressly disclaims responsibility of the content herein.

Human Essays: Conscripted Poems 1971-2021

Published by Gatekeeper Press
2167 Stringtown Rd, Suite 109
Columbus, OH 43123-2989
www.GatekeeperPress.com

Copyright © 2021 by Paul Gillespie
All rights reserved. Neither this book, nor any parts within it may be sold or reproduced in any form or by any electronic or mechanical means, including information storage and retrieval systems without permission in writing from the author. The only exception is by a reviewer, who may quote short excerpts in a review.

Library of Congress Control Number: 2020952273

ISBN (paperback): 9781662907180
eISBN: 9781662907197

For Cooper, Aiyisha, Saysan, and Jamila

CONTENTS

I. Starting Points
Anatidae Caballus 3
Greystoke 4
Monkey 5
Once Upon a Time in the Bathroom 6
Ascent 7
Sleepy Hollow 8
Getting Laid 9
Goya 10
Abscission 11
Gift 12
Heirloom 13
Short Story 14
Epithalamium for Tom and Donna 15
The Ants Have Me 17
The Modern 18
Claudia 19
Birth 20
Cost 21
Mine 22
The Cool White 23

II. On Foreign Ground
Flying to Bangkok 27
Airline Pilot 28
V 29

Everywhere 30
The Villages Are Emptying 32
In the Terminal 33
James 34
Lao Airways 35
The Cemetery 36
No Believer 37
Sunny 39
We Fought 43
What Is Time 44
Regret 45
The Emptying 46
Statues 47

III. Molded

What We Are Left With 51
Casting 52
Old Ron 53
Salsa Lessons 54
Only Lunch 55
Shan 56
Never Taking the Time 57
The Enemy 58
Colorful Corals 59
Most Sensitive 60
Once Was New 61
Three Particles 62
Kyla Long Ago 63

She Is Cool	65
What Do You Remember	66
Passages	67
Chances	68
The End of The Hunt	70
Ubi Sunt	71
Robert	72
August 2018	73
Holly	74
Strands	75
I Used to Hold You Like This	76
On the Trail	77
Pandemic Blues	78
Molded	79
Acknowledgments	80

I
Starting Points

ANATIDAE CABALLUS

Old Caroline was a stockroom manager in one of those
ancient, run-down, perpetually broken Kresge's stores.
And every morning she'd plop her round cone of a body
down at the fountain, crunch chrysanthemums and
chomp-chew-chug
                a donut
                       and coffee
licking the last little pieces of sugar, shining
like small snowflakes
                (and also the dirt
                              and grease)
from her thin web-wrinkly fingers.
And then she'd waddle off and blow kisses of flowers
at us all day
        through her galloping gums.

GREYSTOKE

My lady,
I cannot love you as Buddha might love,
nor as ol' Donald Juan so undoubtedly could have,
and sorry, kid, not like John Alden uneasily didn't;
young Cyrano de Bergerac's nose might have blown for you,
                                                                                                      but

as I come swinging through trees, my butt bouncing off chimpanzees,
tough luck,
        'cause you stuck with me,
                        Jane.

MONKEY

Now there's a monkey on my back,
With a knack for what I lack,
Reminding me to pack

Away the stories in the stack,
Because what matters most, in fact,
And all that's left to track,

Which surest subtleties attack,
The festered fading into black,
Is this monkey on my back.

ONCE UPON A TIME IN THE BATHROOM

A round, thirsty bug rolled up and died
upon my sandstone floor. I found his passing
body, like an eon in a fetal
hiding place, and wrapped him in a careful
piece of tissue paper, coffin
for a toilet burial.
He flushed away to find eternity,
while only I was sad.

ASCENT

The final candle glows,
Its swanlike movements sow
Hints of passing, graceful strength.
A halo wraps the length
Of this incessant friend
To angel's woes, and ends
In glistened azure night
And melted wax scent—light
In violet drops that fall
A heavenly distance. Tall
Caressing point, it is
A spire's arisen kiss
To wings; and into this
Glow dreams flown far away,
And swirling feathers pray.

SLEEPY HOLLOW

two old, never-smiling men
with monkey mouths asleep,
sitting in a bus station passing
sandwiches between them like
bananas under beckett lights,
one leans against the other with an all
important words-before-the-dawn look
and says, "the train arrives in fifteen
minutes." but certainty is certainly not,
so perhaps it's two o'clock THIS
morning traveling on an afterthought
and all along you're wondering why
while pacing the empty ticket booth
with tunnel vision,
telling you you're
in the wrong place;
dadadadadada
jamais vous?

GETTING LAID

You're almost there, while passing through the whorehouse door
one violent night to find persuasive promises,
just scantily introduced and paraded around the floor.
You pick your pleasure party, make your purchases,
and steal away with loneliness to learn that you're
the greatest lover, slicing sterling bills between
your bodies, being almost there, but wanting more,
the beauty of the image lilting, like the lean
enchanted palms of misty apparitions, draped
in silence, always there, but not for those who'd love
her. And Stravinsky keeps repeating that he's raped
her, coming just a little closer, but above
us still; Da Vinci, Michelangelo, Rafael:
their paintings pass through cracking centuries
and hang unfinished still, and almost there. So tell
the swiftly tangled words, as if the miseries
of hands that wrote were grasping, feeling they were there,
but not quite: they could hear and form the words, still. Bared,
the clothes come on again, and trying not to care,
and almost there, but never quite, for though we've shared
our nakedness, the hurried fact is, as we part,
concealed: we know little of that brooding sty
of vessels that surrounds each other's hidden heart,
and having come so skindeep close, which is why,
while driving off, you miss her. You had missed her long
before you came, when laying longing in delay
with silent joys and sorrows. You will always long
and miss her, after having come so far away.

GOYA

The Spanish aristocrats whispered,
"A middling portrait painter at best, certainly no Velasquez."
But there was a war. There's always a war.
Napoleon cruises into Spain, all bullshit about
liberation and new ideas, but he's really hot
for torture and death,
and a middling portrait painter
paints *The Third of May*, and wanders
the countryside, sketchbook in hand,
etching, in black and white (which are really shades of gray)
cataloging cruelty: women raped, dead bodies, blood, starvation,
dismemberment, mutilations mounted on trees,
capturing the suffering,
the horror: *The Disasters of War*.
The middling portrait painter
becomes something else entirely.
Artist,
       Great.

ABSCISSION

it had to be done after the watermelon season,
swaddled in chorion and blood, pulprind and seed,
waking to black flak and falling out of a socketless sky
to land
dead
in the emptying breath of existence.
the nightmare gunner,
once alive, but little more and
mostly possibilities.
accident and choice, both are now cut.
(i have no sense of it; only woman can,
and who am i?)
she is left alone to close the wound,
deeper than flesh,
and in dissonant cities everywhere
daughters living in glassware are
mourning their (just freshly slipped
from the vinebelly of life)
stone children
too.

GIFT

my mother once gifted me a picture,
smelling of her cigarette smoke and sentimentality,
of a sheepishly grinning cartoon tiger,
which represented the happiness she found
in her childhood. i couldn't find mine in it,
amidst the broken doors, holes punched into walls,
profanities strewn like fractured glass.
my father has collapsed on the living room floor,
unconscious in his hurt and fury,
and i am ten again,
running down the dirt road in the dark for help,
"my father is dying" i say over and over to myself,
sobbing

HEIRLOOM

Grandma died leaving me eight hundred dollars
and a TV set. The doctors cut off her hands and feet
(gangrene they said, and next would come the arms and legs)
wanting more, but the old man, her son,
hair combed straight back in resolution,
(I truly believed as a boy there was nothing he couldn't do)
said no, let her go.

And so she did, still looking human, with drugged,
leaking eyes, unable to make the final decision.

I remember the last time I saw her,
before the sickness,
passing through her tiny apartment for ninety minutes,
enroute to other destinations.
She stood chest high to me in house slippers,
a soft Portuguese cylinder
with a gleaming grin perched in a pumpkin head,
smiling from crowsfeet-laughing eyes that couldn't see me,
stuffing a dollar in my hand like I was four and
smelling like lilacs again.

SHORT STORY

In Sparks, where there weren't any creating hope,
in the shadows of his rusting trailer,
reeking of bacon grease and dirt,
old man stink and piss,
Pall Malls, whiskey,
                          the past,
sitting on cheap plastic kitchen furniture,
my railroad grandfather told me about
his French whore he'd spent days and perfumed nights with
after the Great War, the one with trenches and mustard gas
and legions of futile dead.
But she had wanted to get married and
that was how French whores got to America in those days,
he speculated, divorcing the soldier after arriving.
He saw her on the streets of San Francisco while
hurrying off to work one morning years later,
so she must have pulled that trick
on some other unsuspecting doughboy,
he says, and that was the last time he saw her,
climbing onto a cable car in hasty comme-tallez-vous sentences.
How life turns
                out

EPITHALAMIUM FOR TOM AND DONNA

Let me fall in love again,
       The golden sun's delight,
With you.
Let me dance a dancer's dream
Of you
(The old and new).
Our cabriole and pirouettes,
The movements true,
The we are one
And we are two
(And old and new).

Let me fall in love again,
       The shadowed, sleepless night,
With you.
Let me promises redeem
For you
(The old and new).
Now lives restrained with daily tests
       And questions cue,
The why am I
And I am who
(And old and new).

Let me fall in love again
       Betrothed, in wedding-white,
With you.
Let me speak again my vows that seem

To you
(The borrowed and the blue)
But whispered, passionate requests
      And promise new,
The this is me
And this is you,
I do, I do.

THE ANTS HAVE ME

The ants have me.
I have stomped and crushed their noisy
legions flat into the carpet. I have sprayed
Raid throughout the corners and cracks
of the room, and watch carefully for every lone
scout, extinguishing his certain life unmercifully.

But in bed, at night, in the dark,
closing my eyes to seek the relief
of sleep and dreams,
I feel them tingling at my feet, clawing
my leg hairs. Their armies are climbing, crawling up
my legs! Then, ripping off the sheets I find,
switching on the light, screaming! Twitching! I find,
the bed empty.
The ants have me.

THE MODERN

The height of modern architecture,
its end result, you see,
simplifying to essence,
all straight lines, steel framework,
aluminum walls, and concrete floors,
saddled with neither adornment, nor affectation,
only the minimum, only the useful,
machine for a machine—the
most functional building in existence,
without emotion, devoid of messy aesthetic.
Behold:
the aircraft hangar.

CLAUDIA

Perhaps you'll read this, wondering who I am,
or recall a drunken apology,
a methodical tautology,
curious if I'm the same man.

Will you remember electrical hands
and soapbox stands,
razored icicles,
hamburger honchos,
and sugar-packet plans?

But perhaps you'll wonder, obscurely chaste,
momentary thoughts lost in fleeting haste,
a face you thought you saw at the corners of a crowd,
a voice that grates on others' ears, exhaling boasts too loud,
recalling desert dunes and cactuses
that formed our teenage past.

And, at last,
perhaps you'll use this as the lining for your garbage can,
                                        bird's pan,
                                        cat's sand.
I don't suppose it matters much,
if matters really do as such.
Ah, but I still love you, Jewish lady,
                        Buddha's baby,
                        peaceful Bahá'í,
and even now, it's not hard to sigh
                                    just why?

BIRTH

one
risk   fear
      challenge   everything   never nothing
and on and on and on and so it goes and so it goes
we are one
         we are two
                 we are three
smiles   laughter   frowns   squalls
and tiny toes resembling mine
only about me to begin with
                 only about you now
                           then
holding as long as lengthways
everything   always
and   endless   possibilities

and yes
always a question mark can i would i could i do i have enough
what about everything i've lived suffered endured do i dare
do i know enough do i care do i can i could i would i   love
oh who are you my oh my oh my oh my oh my
forever?

COST

the price is high,
your gifts not free,
your love expensive, dear,
demanding undying
gratitude of me,
as regularly
you remind me
of your sacrifice,
and my inadequacy.

my love, i've come
to hate your kindness,
my constant cue of weakness
and our trap. i seek
an unheralded opportunity
to thank you, to praise
your thoughtfulness,
but you always
beat me
to the
punch.

MINE

i am watching from the corner of the building,
where you cannot see me.
in the empty schoolyard across the street,
hooded dragonflies,
there are only the two of you, six and three.
the older girl bends to tie the younger one's
shoes, as she watches patiently.
then, the two of you leap up, running
in the vastness of the sand and playground equipment,
laughing and panting in the rhythmic distance,
and
i am crying at your beauty.

THE COOL WHITE

The cool white comes between us,
an incandescent glow, furious, blinding,
the final stage of a sun about to explode,
or collapse in on itself.

"Good morning," I say to her, but it isn't.
Hearing only ourselves, not each other,
distant now, conversations as bad
as the bleached bones of cannibals,
or startled mink eating their young.

We have terrible arguments over technicalities,
somethings, nothings.

The wedding plates are broken,
shards sent off in plastic bags to the dump,
and pictures, cards, letters—
all bagged too, on both sides of us,
our history discounted to a mistake,
torn from quilted betrayal,
our stories as irrelevant
as fiction in the modern world.

The cruel white comes between us
on opposite sides of the room,
chewing up hopes and dreams,
and all the best memories,

leaving only the worst of us behind.

II
ON FOREIGN GROUND

FLYING TO BANGKOK

I was never young, Wayne said.
In the glow of cockpit instruments,
the deep facial furrows and pits of middle age
hinted as much, as we flew our DC-10
in nightblack over Laos and Vietnam. He'd
close his eyes and slip into memory, hearing
the cacophonic staccato of ancient radio traffic,
*taking fire, taking fire, down in the tree line, alpha
one charlie, taking fire*, his ghostly radio crammed
full of voices, hurried, excited, trying to escape
anti-aircraft shells and missiles from below.
He sighed,
*Twenty-three of my friends ended up in the Hanoi Hilton…
and I was never young.* I believed him,
as we'd make routine position reports from our
airliner to old men whispering in the dark
down below us, recounting their lost youth
                                            too.

AIRLINE PILOT

a victim of time zones,
removed from the rhythm of light,
i wake up just before dawn,
lying in the dark of this hotel room,
on the other side of the world, trying
to remember where the bathroom is,
what day it is, what hour, what hotel.
(what i am sure of: outside—oppressive, tropical
heat and humidity). staring
into the mirror, my narrowed vision sees
the furrowed effects of a savage bird of prey
scratching and clawing its way up
my face. reflecting on the things we
do for money, measured in time,
the splitting of seconds, the meeting of schedules,
considering how cheap my
worth, another expendable body
in the financial activities of man;
my ancestors, phoenicians and the
grunt sailors of columbus,
trading precious moments of life
for the cool feel of distant breezes
and the promise of spice.

V

Staring at this wall in the airport, leaving,
thinking of you last night, smile on smile,
kiss on kiss, eyes in eyes, and holding
you as full as touch, your secrets, my stories.

Then this morning, having spoken on the
phone, we laughed but still I couldn't persuade you
to be Laura to my Zhivago, words on words. So
I am staring at this wall, feeling foolish,

eyes in eyes, and lost, as empty as beige.
Brick by brick, chest on chest, our worlds
stretch, collide in different directions, parting.
Memory: arms and legs entangled like vines.

Now the careful, measured responsibilities,
stone on stone, of former promises to keep,
hands in hands, but smell, but taste, but touch
stay, and I am staring at this wall.

EVERYWHERE

everywhere
            you are
                        everywhere
i drift within these airports, strange,
our fingers moving out of range,
your kiss still tasted, silent tear,
your breath a whisper i yet hear.
our worlds collide then fade apart
inside my shaken, swollen heart,
our last goodbye still vibrating
a rending, wanting, violent thing.
your scented sweat, your skin my soul,
within your eyes i find my whole;
but wind and sun and sky my home,
as night meets day and day is gone
(i should go? or will you stay
with me? a question i'm afraid to pray)
the echo of your elegance,
your love the precious gift of chance
or fate? life's meaning fractured by seconds split
and pressing schedules made to fit.

everywhere
        you are
                everywhere
while distances divide us, dear,
this wandering future now and here,
you're wondering what words are true?
          i
am moving through these forests, through
these fields, through these towns,
a stranger to these people who surround
(your face in every fleeting look,
that scan or staring overtook)
me, present, but not truly such,
familiar to your kindest touch,
but foreign in this land,
and everywhere you are
                my love
                      i am

THE VILLAGES ARE EMPTYING

the villages are emptying,
the young men thrown in jail
for cutting down the imported eucalyptus
trees that suck the moisture from the earth,
scourge of crops and farmers,
leaving hard-baked clay.
the young women have gone south,
indentured (willingly and not)
by their fathers, for a new Toyota, or
motorbike, traded for sex. everyone pretends
ignorance, and everyone knows.

and we come, farang, from across
oceans of christian privilege and prurience,
driven by extremes, excited by their
brown nakedness and soft availability, arriving
from failed familial ties with our
middle-aged bellies, shriveled balls and sagging cocks,
farmer's tans lusting for youth,
and they our dollars, trained from buddhist birth
to accept their inevitability, we resisting ours,
soulless, like the trees forced upon them, we
leave only parched, aching earth behind.

IN THE TERMINAL

She plies him with her smooth brown skin,
the color of earth, the texture of Thai silk,
here in public, holding his hand, or letting
his hands roam around her body,
which no good Thai girl would ever do
(the other women waiting, steal furtive
disapproving glances at the faux lovers).
She is working. He has bought her a ticket
to Chiang Mai, and her time, but
American, in his baseball cap, tennis shoes and shorts,
he thinks they are falling in love.

JAMES

James,
face framed in his long, yellow strung-out hair,
talks of cultural relativism, ecology, values.
the mystifying nature of Thai society,
the spiritual and familial struggles of his Thai girlfriend,
unknowable ultimately, he tells me.
I let him be the expert, and don't
tell him about the rules of hierarchical cultures,
dust and the bumpiness of the road enveloping us,
or how the famous Thai smile masks the whole
panoply of savage human emotions,
fear, disgust, frustration, anger.
Chai yen, they say, but every heart knows these things.
He is young still, and intelligent, living
on a precipice here and riding in this songtao,
gone,
wrapped in a sarong, his feet bituminous with
dirt and fungus,
wondering if he shouldn't be taking on
some responsibilities and
making money.
His teeth are turning black as he speaks,
perfecting the fine art of staring into space,
lost.

LAO AIRWAYS

In the Chinese turboprop
there is no safety briefing.
I motion to the tiny wrinkled grandmother
next to me how to buckle her seat belt,
but she grins, waves me carelessly away.
What is to know now?
She's been in war, been bombed by B-52s,
given birth in a hut many times,
and dismissed, or hid from, or survived
tiger, krait, fire, malaria, dengue, cobra, communist.
The monsoons come, the monsoons go.
Through missing teeth
she smiles merrily at this adventure,
and as we soar high over jungle and rice paddies
she remains free from constraint.

THE CEMETERY

We walked into the Catholic cemetery on Silom,
because you liked reading the headstones,
imagining the lives lived,
underneath, beneath the granite.

Hidden in the din of traffic and endless construction of high-rises,
it was being moved for a new building,
the remains of over a hundred years relocated,
and they were being very careful with the remains,
the workmen said, who pounded down the markers and stones
with sledgehammers.

But,
wandering through this last disintegrating island of the dead
in modern Bangkok,
we found a concrete coffin, holes in its sides and top.

Peering in we could see the jumbled
bones of vanished souls, amid stagnant rainwater and mud,
counting (of varying sizes) seven skulls.

NO BELIEVER

I am no believer,
no crucifix surrounds my throat,
no holy bibles by the bed,
no chants to absent saviors, rote,
or afterlife alms placed for dead.
I am no believer,
no sad Jew has died for my sins,
imagining some new chance begins.
No suffering raja's meditation
defines my daily destination
or tortured path to self-negation.
But here at night in agitation,
full moon above, my love away,
as she walks through fields of war
and desperate refugees, I pray
    May god protect and guide her,
    please bring her home to me.

I am no believer,
no temples hold my reasoned heart,
and I affirm no prophecy.
But rather, in kindness let us start,
not indulgence nor tithe money.
And I am no believer,
no desert prophet leadeth me,
his family in constant anarchy,
nor any shepherd's Yahweh professing
His the Only way. Confessing:

in this cool darkness, feeling
my anxious heart's erratic beating
for my lover's distant day,
where moaning women starve in sunlight,
men's limbs are hacked away, I pray
    May god protect my love tonight,
    please bring her home to me.

I am no believer
in praise of wars of endless vengeance,
that leave no cruelty to chance,
where zealots shed blood of innocents,
as casually as smashing ants.
I am no believer,
my thinking gets me through the day,
and whispered words that lovers say.
I place my trust in trees and flowers,
reflections passed in quiet hours.
But roadside bombs and scattered snipers,
the murdering stealth of human vipers,
where uncleared furtive minefields lay
in bleak lament my fearful sight,
marasmic children huddle, and I pray
    May god protect my true love tonight,
    please bring her home to me.

SUNNY

The worst was hours wrenching into days, wrapped
deep within the darkened forest jungle,
teak, palmyra, tamarind, bamboo trees
morphing into evergreens, my soldiers
stretching me over the border to Mae Sot and
doctors, every shifting balance kindling
pain, my spine warped, twisting like a
banded krait, the vertebra cracked, and I—
helpless, paralyzed observer to its
movement. We never saw the mortar round
(sixty millimeter, one-twenty?) that spared me,
leaving others dying, legs or arms
ripped away, or shredded. I
recall the sun-sprinkled moment, lifted
by concussion, flying through the morning
backward, slamming like a locust in a
gale, against the bark that broke my back. And
after seven years, it was done for
me, our war, replaced by learning how to
walk and sit and bend again. Beyond my
body's pain, though, what I hated most was
never being fit to join my men
again, my brave Karen emerald warriors.

Growing up in Rangoon, I never learned the
language of my people, Sgaw, Pwo—
English and Burmese instead. My mum would
always say, "The Burmese have a saying:
'Wind blows in where fire rages.'"

                              Ending the
promise of democracy and homeland,
when I was in university, the
SLORC began the persecution of our
ethnic peoples. Entering the villages, the
Tatmadaw first would shoot the cows, the
dogs, the buffalo, and beat the pleading
owners and their wives, searching through the
thatch-roofed huts for rice, curry pots,
valuables, then torching homes and crops,
raping every woman, even old aunties and
children: soft, brown, thanaka-covered
cheeks melting in the flames; screams
mingling in the humid heat with buzzing
cicadas and beating dragonfly wings. At
twenty-three, my mum crying, I joined the
KNU; I went to war. The Burmese
have a saying
            "Follow any path, you
come to a village at the end."

The line of our single-file army, like the
curves of a cobra, wound sinuously over
hills and streams and rice paddies, past the termite
mounds, mosquitos, and flies; our only sound the
clink of metal or straps, the clatter of muted
flip-flops. Out-gunned, out-manned, our war was fought like we
fired our M-16s, single-shot, never on
automatic, to save the bullets, and keep the
barrels from melting. Rising through the ranks,
I became a captain. My men were brave; we
shared the stinky fish paste and rice, blood,

insects, sweat, malaria, dengue, and, late at
night, laughter, though I was always careful
as their leader, not to laugh too loud—they
needed my detachment, patience, firmness, and
knew that I might have to sacrifice
one for all, and yes, I did.
For a time Americans came, bringing
weapons, training; teaching us to march
or parachute, or scuba in the Salween (imagine!),
But the Salween River will never dry, a
buffalo's horn will never be straight, another
place, another war, and they left.

When the monsoons came, walls of windswept,
flooding water formed dripping jungles,
swollen rivers, swamped crop fields,
soggy villages, mildewed soldiers.

Roads and trails became impassable
canals of mud sludge (we'd ride the surer
feet of elephants, then), day after day as
gray as the dead bodies lying in the
orchid ambush fields. Moment of truth,
moment of fear; every soldier's war the
same. The Burmese have a saying,
                        "Once you
have known death, you come to know the price of a
coffin."

Our endless war (forty years?
fifty? sixty?) squandered generations,
believing that the hair of a golden cat would

fend off the danger from a tiger, victims not only
of the Tatmadaw, but also the
corruption of our leaders, Bo Mya's ministers
trading teak, pyinkado, padauk with
Burmese generals, their children at expensive
private schools overseas. And our
inertia. Not every arrow strikes its target, and
cut water leaves no mark. Where do we go
from here, we the vanquished, our women, children,
old, now running like chickens or ring-wormed rats,
squatting fearful in the jungle, hiding,
foraging, escaping rape, torture,
slavery, extermination. The upper
body begs from the sun, the lower body
begs from the stars, and we are left to beg from
strangers, scattered like pine needles or rice chaff in the
wind, to Australia, America, Europe,
or the refugee camps, facing Thai
beatings and extortion. Beyond a bend in the
river, we can see, beyond a bend in the
sea, we cannot.

    Who knows of our
sorrow, charred remains of villages,
abandoned crop fields, grief of our daughters,
murdered children? I am Ko Ko Thein, and I
am Karen. I fought in a war of which few
know, and fewer care, against tyranny, for
freedom, our culture, for a home to call our
own, Kawtholei, "A land without
evil," and most of all, our human
                        right.

WE FOUGHT

we fought, i left.
i floated down into depths
weightless, breathing purified air,
and came across small
mounds of mollusk shells.
outside an octopus hole,
i find you,
your colors, rust and brown.
you cannot see this,
but my love is here,
floating in this teal sea.
it guides me
to the surface,
always.

WHAT IS TIME

What is time?
My life has been framed in smell.
We drifted, we lay there for days,
naked in heat and moisture,
the banana tree out our window
a sentinel canopy; eucalyptus
wafted through the morning
as hummingbirds stole the blush
from bougainvillea
(but scorpions and venomous orange centipedes
scurried in the underbrush),
and I became lost in orchids,
living on air, deep
                      breathing.

Jasmine,
I dream I am your lover again,
in the darkened teak rice barn,
waking beneath the mosquito net over your bed,
inhaling in the sheets
scent of your cunt and underarms,
spoor of your juices and my semen
caking my cock,
hearing the roosters who have
crowed all night, succumbing to cicadas,
your voice an aria to the sunrise,
bouquet of your perfume
a trail to the door,
your long, dark hair vanishing through it,
escaping me.

REGRET

Wanting so much more and finding less,
there is so much to say, no space contains
it. What you did was not just curious,
but with excuse, reflection strains and stains
(as if your passions justified your choices)
our intimacy, leaving hopelessness,
and pivoting intrusion now of other voices.
Wanting so much more, and finding less.

THE EMPTYING

Our pool of faith,
filled from the deepest wellsprings of hope,
now unreplenished,
a tepid floating abattoir of irrevocable sorrow,
blood and marrow,
as you move through the house,
a stranger with boundaries.
Most painful of destinations,
our stark bedroom dry and cavernous, echoing
volcanic conversations we will never have,
conducted in deafening silences.
No promises exist in polite brief waves,
and no possibilities,
only the cracking ache of tearless goodbye.
Leaving, I search my bags in vein
for something you might have left me,
a card, a candy, your heart,
finding only memory.
There is nowhere to turn,
from this love misplaced,
and our dreams ripple away from us,
vanishing into air

STATUES

On Avenue Louise in Brussels,
past the statues of urinating children and
monuments to colonization, is a statue
of a naked African with a chain around his ankle,
holding his small child, pleading upward in agony
for relief from the two Malinois
savagely tearing at his legs.
When erected, this was meant to show
the humanitarian largess of King Leopold, who
proclaimed he was releasing the black from slavery
and bringing freedom and dignity
to the Congo, while his soldiers
raped and pillaged resources, murdering men, women and
children to enhance his wealth
(but now exists
as a testament to the butcher he was).

There are statues throughout the American South,
of Confederate generals—Robert E. Lee, Stonewall Jackson,
Nathan Bedford Forrest—praising their valor, praising
their cause, hailing their example,
whitewashing their truth:
they were traitors, and their cause was slavery.
No more honorific lies.

III
Molded

WHAT WE ARE LEFT WITH

as you lay dying i sat
in the dark, hearing your voice, as gentle as mist.
so this is what we have come to, my dear,
the end of a marriage all tubes and wires and electronics,
the foreign noises of the white jungle,
and this duty, to sit here, to watch, to wait.
i spent the night in this chair,
fading in and out of sleep with you
(the nurses giving me patronizing looks),
wiping your forehead with a cool washcloth,
suctioning saliva and phlegm out of your mouth,
rubbing your arm as a distraction from the pain or
calling the distant nurse for more medicine, another shot.
doctors appeared, and briefed me about bile and livers,
pneumonia and morphine. the clot in your right arm
has caused it to swell up to a carnival size.
there are things i wish i could forget, especially now,
but what i remember here in the early hours of morning
is our love,
and our war.
this is no place to live,
we know, our final journey together,
just you and me.

CASTING

Castabout, my friend.
We were as close as lovers once,
on the other side of our youth,
reeling and drawing, before
wading into our futures.
I look at you now,
a lifetime ago,
searching for a current connection,
a hook to wind you in live,
but you've gone. Your speech
stumbles over the rocks, and
I laugh at all the wrong spots.
All we have producing honest laughter now
is our past, on the shore,
tying flies.

OLD RON

The mentally disabled shuffle by, across the street,
escaping for the day their group home,
hunched over, moving carefully,
very often with different shoes on their feet.
Old Ron, cheeks always stubbled,
smelling of sweat and beer,
stops to talk to me and gather his thoughts.
A grin on his weathered face, he's happy
to tell me about his latest
adventure on the bus or
the fickleness of the weather.
I leave him finally, in the street,
not knowing what else to talk about.
He spends a minute, underneath his
Tigers baseball cap, trying to remember
something, then ambles away to the corner bar,
one foot in front of the other,
having forgotten long ago the bullet
in Vietnam
               that stole his future.

SALSA LESSONS

the other, your friend,
moves beneath my fingers
like the ballerina she once was,
light as a feather, long, lithe, smooth,
soft to the touch, steady in the movement.
you, though, move like a sock filled with sand,
heavy, immovable. i am dragging you around
the floor like turning wrenches, like stacking firewood.
this is hard, unforgiving, unyielding work.
one dances above, one tries to push through.
at night i was reading your
prose, though (a song of cold, alcoholic, violent
Alaska), forged in your childhood suffering.

ONLY LUNCH

in winter
we meet for lunch
in a small
        buried café
                overhead
the jungle of asphalt caverns and canyons of skyscrapers
thick-cold concrete and steel
seeking warmth and connection huddled together
the whoareyou guarded necessity
and inevitably
i think i hear you
your heart your iron your suffering
parting speechless with nothing in common
i gave you two books of poems
(a desperate act)
that you re-gifted

SHAN

alone in the frightened city,
stalked by the ghosts of dead Parsee,
she waits for the pedigreedmoneyedman--
finance, law or medicine
—who will arrive in his Bentley,
to father her children, set scenery,
only the best will do, only,
perfect, not secondary.

but in the rivers of people
filling the narrowing valleys
of stifling steel and stone,
(so many, how can there be no one)
serial lovers, failed expectations, in her forties,
the pressing desperation of time, empty,
her missing children are weeping,
no one is coming to save us.

NEVER TAKING THE TIME

never taking the time,
never making the effort,
to know another person, really know,
their first kiss and snowfall, fear and loss.
what do you want today,
                        tomorrow,
                                      in ten years?
such a rare, perilous, precious event,
casually dismissed in the hubris
and invincibility of youth,
thinking there would be many more occasions
to repeat connections,
in age finding only
a few, and then,
none.

the enemy is air—the oxygen we need to live destroys us.

colorful corals collapse, destroyed by carbon, warming oceans, man.

eyes, most sensitive to greens, measure the seasons, food, beauty, danger.

once was new, was truth,
certainty enveloped doubt,
but always a lie.

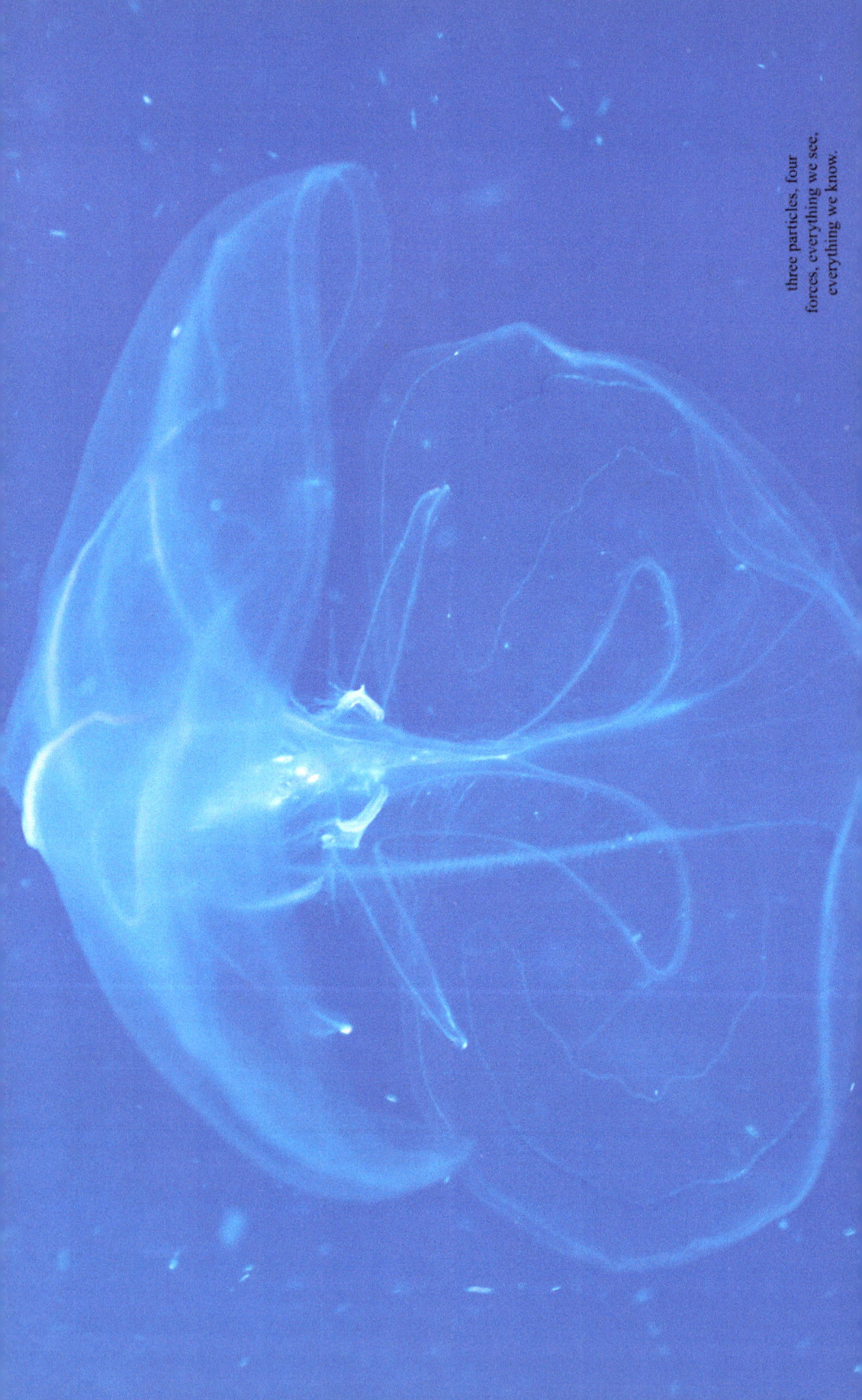

three particles, four forces, everything we see, everything we know.

KYLA LONG AGO

It's long ago now, what we shared,

          but I remember

                    pacing your loneliness,

our walls smelled like airplanes

                of oil, grease, gasoline

                          and

distance.

How many mornings many did you sleep naked,

              while I longed for you,

humming in the sunrise with the freedom of flight

(kissing its vastness and fear with cool objectivity)...

time slipped by for me as carelessly as clouds,

swathed in the stale taste of airport vending machines

                      cigarettes, caffeine,

broken sleep....

How many days many did I sweat in the power blast of blue sky

    while you whispered weeks for me to our

                      daughter,

in my absence, loyal to my presence,

"daddy's flying helicopters, daddy's flying airplanes,"

and

we

waited, like prayers....

And how many nights many was our only speech the tired

warmth of

        sleeping bodies and droning engine dreams,

and my promise,

I'll be home soon, my love.

SHE IS COOL

she is cool to the read, distant. Eastern.
examine my words, she says, my art
floats above, without me.
so down, down i'm drawn
into the gray overcast
with my foggy northwest questions.
i jump into the hypothermic water, immerse myself
in exacting precision, carefully drawn observations,
lacking violence or fear or rage. but
something's missing. i pull hand over hand
down the long, bulbous, floating kelpwords,
pushing aside leaves of metaphors and
promises, seeking the roots,
the attachment points to substrate.
arriving on the bottom sitting
with the old crabs, her tendrils
only drift above me, connected
to nothing tangibly and
no one.

WHAT DO YOU REMEMBER

What do you remember,
What did you forget?
Smells of her September,
What do you remember?
Painful in December,
Sad, the reason of regret.
What do you remember,
What did you forget?

Parting, wistful ember,
Mind's now nimble reset,
Memories dismember,
Parting wistful ember.
Old remains the splendor,
Gracefully sung duet,
Parting wistful ember,
Mind's now nimble reset.

PASSAGES

In winterlust, drunk on wine and snow,
With Linda driving over Bishop Pass,
Her breasts beneath my touch adagio,
Our operatic passion never fast.

So time a construct, warped by mass and speed,
And Holly's throaty laugh and softest kiss
Since lost to moving flashbacks' fleeting seed,
The moment's frozen movements, captured bliss.

In mountains seconds speed, black holes they stop,
Veroni's singing bringing in my morn,
Her melodies caressed memories crop,
Amid the breathless orchids, I'm reborn.

As time constricts I hold their passing face
And clutch the fading, folded moments' grace.

CHANCES

The chances taken, and their cost,
the mountain pass to fertile ground,
the risks taken, and then lost,
uncertain path through woods to sound.

The waves wash in, the waves wash out,
never certain what we're about.
I'm thinking fast, I'm thinking slow,
never sure which way to go.

On the fluid shore,
what do you want, were you asking?
Bumbling, stumbling, tumbling choice,
descending in to act.
Outside the apartment,
I'm hunched over in the dark,
wet in the rain tapping on your driver's window,
"Can we talk, please? I don't want you to sleep in your car."
But no, the window stays up,
boundary to your heart, stony, forward facing.
You wait until I've gone to bed to return,
and in the morning I see your closed door.
All the stones we've stepped are overturned,
all the stories we've shared silent,
plans scattered like driftwood,
every touch poison.

The waves wash in, the waves wash out,
never certain what we're about.
I'm thinking fast, I'm thinking slow,
never sure which way to go.

The unwanted kiss I gave too soon,
the longing too-long hug I stole,
returning in the afternoon,
you were gone, and I would know.

THE END OF THE HUNT

At Ephesus, I was
merely a tourist taking pictures,
and never knew her hidden heart,
the crippled carpet-seller's wife,
my concierge, what she'd lost and what remained.

My favorite place is the Temple of Artemis, she says.
But there's nothing there, I protest, one of the
Wonders of the Ancient World reduced to a lonely
broken column, stagnant pools, a swamp.

Ah, but look closer, she says, woven in moonglow.
Essence remains: turtles sunning on the rocks,
a stork on the pillar,
swans gliding in the water,
the muted ghost of Artemis renewing.
There are births, there are deaths, the seasons reflect in the water
(Heraclitus sleeps below, unreadable, unpredictable),
and
    change.

UBI SUNT

The animals are dying, where are they?
The oceans come acidic, did you hear?
The ends untying surely, turn away.

More babies born, more smoke-emitted day,
Incautious, selfish shepherds of our sphere,
The animals are dying, where are they?

The rising stormy waters drown the bay,
And rivers flood the cities every year,
The ends untying surely, turn away.

No coral reefs, no mammals here one day,
Without the swifted fright, there is no fear.
The animals are dying, turn away.

The silent strands of nature we'll obey,
Removing threaded comforts we hold dear,
The ends untying surely, turn away.

Through missing truths remiss and lies, we sway,
Ignoring what is known, what is near,
The animals are dying, where are they?
The ends surely untying, turn away.

ROBERT

We were friends once, sharing stories
of ex-wives and lovers, angry mothers

and passive fathers, taking trips to DC, LA, or Seattle,
sharing steaks, laughter, wine and stumbling home.

Before I realized you didn't read books or newspapers,
finding your information on the internet

from videos created by murky organizations
with agendas. This is weird and bitter weather now,

opaque clouds, empty promises.
What you hold dear, the pillars you're embracing

are crumbling cement to me, cached conspiracies,
convoluted canards,

what you believe in your core, and what is
lost to you: science, logic, reason,

the Enlightenment. Your definition
of truth, honesty, fairness—not mine.

How can I talk to you through the fog?
We choose what we choose to see.

My black stepdaughter and her black husband
have lifetimes of experienced racism,

but you, German white, said to me,
America is not a racist country.
And in a moment, we ended.

AUGUST 2018

The lighthouse light blinks
on and off across the bay through the haze,
lights from the houses on the ridge above winking
on in the dimming twilight, and a handful
of sailboats in the still air,
find their way home under motor.

The smoke envelops the trees, the hundreds
of wildfires in British Columbia,
hot products of climate change,
have sent their residue south
throughout the state.
In the atmosphere, we are all connected.

Barely moving, scarcely breathing,
summer holding its breath, crushes our days like
fat, old, angry Grendel sitting on our chests,
and the nights are spent sweating in the cooler downstairs,
with electric fans firing on high,
the only movement inside the house.

HOLLY

Pistil and stamen, as tremulous as passion,
wanting you, vibrating, when nothing is hoped for,
nor promised. Spiderwebs stretch between our
stalks to others, collecting their daily due, while
the memory of kissing you blows on the wind,
naked, fumbling with hooks and clothes,
without the time,
                    only by chance
to create the pain of other men.

Not protected by your sepal, your parents
abdicating that role early and often,
now your petals flowing outward, blossom.
The sun's heat swallows our afternoons,
its light probing every inch of color,
every moment of skin we share,
without the time,
                    only by chance
to create the pain of other men.

I leave to fly, we've only days, and
wrenched to tears of loss months later,
carried on the wind, moving through the world
and attached to all the sticky strands collected, like you.
I learn later that you die at 43, kidney disease,
and I regret nothing, our accident,
without the time,
                    only by chance
to create the pain of other men.

STRANDS

The strands of community
woven across our doors,
like spiders' webs,
a fragile latticework
of time and words and feelings,
so easily cast adrift when
one strand becomes detached.
Certainty is certainly not:
to know a thing and its other,
all in the same heartbeat.
Jeremy's friend committed suicide
two weeks ago and
he still doesn't know quite what to say,
without sounding inadequate or clichéd.

I USED TO HOLD YOU LIKE THIS

Schizophrenia has taken over your brain,
coloring your perceptions in paranoid

delusions, and endless repetitive self-dialogues.
Friendships have escaped, jobs are lost,

and family avoids you. Confusion, hurt and anger
betray your potential.

But today I walk to the couch and sit next to you,
encircling you in my arms, and you mold into me.

I used to hold you like this
when you were a child,

on my lap, close,
melted chocolate against my chest.

Thank you, whispers the earth,
for your movement.

Thank you, says the flower,
for your love.

Thank you, whistles the sky,
for your thought.

Thank you, murmurs the water,
for your heart.

I used to hold you like this
when you were a child.

ON THE TRAIL

i sit outside the tent on a rock,
surrounded by the forested mountains and rock-bed streams.
i eat lentils and couscous for dinner,
survey the wildflower meadows,
and sleep fitfully on an air mattress.

i eat instant oatmeal in the morning,
my mind blank, listening to silence.
it was difficult getting here, pacing slower than the
younger hikers who scramble over the shale and granite
stones littering the trails, like two-legged mountain goats.

i'm most like an animal here,
in these towering hemlocks, spruce, and fir,
and carefully pick my footfalls traveling.
tearing down the camp and lifting the fifty pounds
of it to my back, i travel quickly now, too quickly.

rounding a curve, fifteen feet away a black bear stands
in the trail, looks at me, then ambles off into the brush.
the cascading ferns hide him, while i
click my hiking sticks together, and
breathing deeply the clear mountain air, move on.

PANDEMIC BLUES

Pacing the wooden floors
or staring out the windows to the sea,
listening for life on the other side of the walls,
a cough, the TV, a toilet flush.
On the computer staying visually
connected to friends and family,
streaming movies and series or
reading books, confined and alone.
I used to travel the world; now
only to the grocery store, masked,
to protect from a creature that can't be seen.
The day to day monotony, what to cook
when to sleep, when to walk, and wine,
missing hugs and conversations, touch.
What once defined us were our possibilities,
now it's our vulnerability.

MOLDED

Molded in the washed-out memory near
Old doors we've passed through, we find
The secrets to our future loom,
In the silent must of empty rooms,
In the peeling paint of abandoned walls, cast
The future always part of the past,
Goodbye always a part of hello,
What we take with us when we go,
The people we love, the things that we know.
Where are you now, but here?
And what was left behind?

ACKNOWLEDGMENTS

The poem Anatidae Caballus was originally published in *Icarus, A Magazine of Creative Writing*, by the United States Air Force Academy Department of English, April 1971.

Two phrases from the poem Abscission, "waking to black flak", and "the nightmare gunner", owe a debt of gratitude to Randall Jarrell's "The Death of the Ball Turret Gunner".

I'd like to thank Karen K. Craigo, whose editing, thought, and commentary were invaluable in the final manuscript.

And special thanks to Gatekeeper Press and Nicole Dudley for shepherding the project.

And then I must thank my mentor, teacher, and friend Dr. Thomas Murawski, who always encouraged us with the adage, *Books are your friends!* I'm grateful, always, for your insights, humor, and wisdom, but deeply resent your ability to out-hike me.

Finally, I'd like to thank Kyla, for four wonderful sources of discovery, our children, and V, who showed me the world, and always inspires.

www.ingramcontent.com/pod-product-compliance
Lightning Source LLC
LaVergne TN
LVHW051225070526
838200LV00057B/4614